BEGINNING HISTORY

VIKING
EXPLORERS

Rupert Matthews

Illustrated by Jack Keay

BEGINNING HISTORY

The Age of Exploration
The American West
Crusaders
Egyptian Farmers
Egyptian Pyramids
Family Life in World War II
Greek Cities
The Gunpowder Plot
Medieval Markets
Norman Castles

Plague and Fire
Roman Cities
Roman Soldiers
Saxon Villages
Tudor Sailors
Tudor Towns
Victorian Children
Victorian Factory Workers
Viking Explorers
Viking Warriors

All words that appear in **bold** are explained in the glossary on page 22.

Series and book editor: Rosemary Ashley
Designer: Helen White

First Published in 1989 by Wayland (Publishers) Limited
61 Western Road, Hove, East Sussex, BN3 1JD.

British Library Cataloguing in Publication Data
Matthews, Rupert
Viking explorers
1. Voyages by Viking longships
I. Title II. Series
910.4'5

HARDBACK ISBN 1-85210-775-8

PAPERBACK ISBN 0-7502-0523-7

Typeset by Kalligraphics Limited, Horley, Surrey.
Printed in Italy by G. Canale & C.S.p.A.
Bound in Belgium by Casterman S.A.

CONTENTS

VIKING VOYAGES

The Vikings lived in **Scandinavia** in the countries of Norway, Sweden and Denmark, about a thousand years ago. Before about 750 most Vikings stayed at home. They grew crops and herded cattle, sheep and goats. Then they began to travel abroad. The Vikings explored large areas of land and sea. Some sailed to Britain and Northern France. They attacked the people living in these countries and stole their wealth.

Other Vikings voyaged across the huge Atlantic Ocean. They settled in desolate lands such as Iceland and Greenland. Other routes took them into eastern Europe and Asia.

A Viking ship battles its way across the Atlantic Ocean.

We do not know why the Vikings started to travel abroad. Perhaps their farms could not provide enough food for them all. Or perhaps they became weary of life at home and wanted to take advantage of the wealth of other lands. Whatever the reasons, the Vikings became the most adventurous explorers of their time.

VIKING SHIPS

The homelands of the Vikings were very mountainous. The easiest way to travel between villages was by water. So the Vikings became skilled at building ships. Their craft were fast, **manoeuvrable** and strong.

Two types of ship were common. The largest was the **longship**, which was used by warriors on raiding expeditions. Longships might be over 30 m long, but only 6 m wide. Shipbuilders always tried to make their ships as beautiful as possible. Large sails were used when the wind was behind the ship. When there was

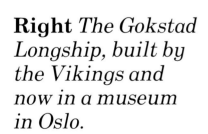

Right *The Gokstad Longship, built by the Vikings and now in a museum in Oslo.*

6

no wind, or it blew in the wrong direction, oars would be used. Filled with up to 80 warriors, the longship was a dangerous weapon in battle. Sometimes a dragon head was carved at the front to make the ship look more frightening.

The second type of ship was the **knarr**. These were smaller and wider than longships. They could carry heavy **cargoes** and were used by **merchants** and farmers.

A Viking nobleman visits the men who are building a ship for him.

NORTHERN ISLANDS

By about the year 800 some Vikings decided to leave Scandinavia to look for new homes. At first they sailed to the Shetland, Orkney and Faroe Islands. These lands were the home of **Celtic** people. But the Vikings took over the islands and started their own farms.

Hunting for small whales off the coast of Iceland.

Soon after this Viking ships sailed out into the open ocean. They found a huge island which was completely empty of people. They called it Iceland because of the glaciers and snows which covered much of the island. At first the Vikings went to Iceland only during the summer. They would fish and hunt whales before going home for the winter.

Later, about the year 900, some Vikings began to settle in Iceland. To reach the island they had to cross vast stretches of stormy sea. It was a dangerous journey, but many Vikings made the voyage for the sake of finding a new home.

Above *A Viking carving showing a ship with a large sail.*

Left *A view of Iceland, showing the lonely landscape of snow-covered mountains and bleak grasslands.*

THE FAR WEST

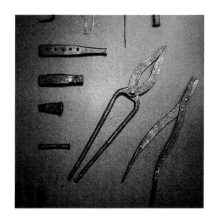

Above *A group of Viking tools recently found in Denmark.*

Viking merchants and farmers often sailed between Iceland and Norway. On one voyage the ship of a man named Gunbjorn was swept far to the west by a terrible storm. Here he sighted a land of mountains and snows. When he reached Iceland, he told everyone about this new land.

In about 960, because of a **feud**, a man named Erik the Red was forced to leave Iceland with all his family. Erik decided to settle in the new land

Right *The rocky coast of Greenland, where many Vikings settled.*

The Vikings visited Vinland (America) to cut down trees for timber.

to the west. He named it Greenland, to make it sound a good place in which to live. It was very cold in Greenland and life was hard for the settlers, but later some 3,000 people joined Erik.

The Vikings from Greenland sailed further west, where they found land that they named **Vinland**. We call this land America. The forests of Vinland provided timber for building houses and ships because there were no trees in Greenland.

LEAVING HOME

The Vikings who explored and settled in the islands of the Atlantic were looking for new lands in which to live. We know that some of these people left homes because they were in trouble. Others set sail because there was not enough land at home for them to farm.

Usually the voyages were made by whole families. Each family took everything they would need to survive in their new home. A ship would be loaded with tools to build a house and farming **implements**, such as ploughs and axes. They also took farm animals, such as cattle, goats and poultry, and seeds for crops. The members of the family would say goodbye to their friends and relatives. Then they would sail westward. Some never returned home, but lived the rest of their lives in the new settlements.

Below *A Viking family set sail on board a knarr to settle in a new land.*

A NEW HOME

Above *A Viking bucket, made of leather with a metal handle.*

The Viking settlers faced difficult tasks. They had to grow enough food for themselves, and produce some goods to sell, in a land never before lived in by humans. The first thing they had to do was to look for good places for their farms. Early settlers needed only to find a suitable place and then they would live there. Ingolf Arnarson, the first settler in Iceland, threw a **sacred** pole from his ship. He built his farm where the pole came ashore. Later settlers

Right *A modern reconstruction of a Viking house, showing the wooden walls and earth floor.*

bought land from those who had arrived earlier.

Once ashore, the farmers had to plough land and plant it with oats and barley. They needed to do this in the spring so that the crop could ripen properly. Then the animals had to be taken to **grazing grounds**. The struggle for survival was very hard. Some settlers gave up and returned to Scandinavia, but most remained. The modern inhabitants of Iceland and other islands are descended from these early Vikings.

Below *A Viking farm on Iceland about the year 1000. Houses were built of stone because wood was rare in Iceland.*

THE GREAT RIVERS

While some Viking explorers sailed west in search of farmland, others travelled east looking for wealth.

They were looking for other nations with which to trade. It was natural for Vikings to travel in their boats, so they nearly always journeyed along the great rivers of eastern Europe.

After finding their way across the Baltic Sea, the Vikings sailed and rowed up the Dvina and Svir rivers. To continue their journeys the explorers had to **portage** their ships. This meant dragging them over dry land to another river. The ships were unloaded to make them as light as possible. Then they were placed on rollers and dragged overland. Oxen and horses might be hired from local villages to help with hauling.

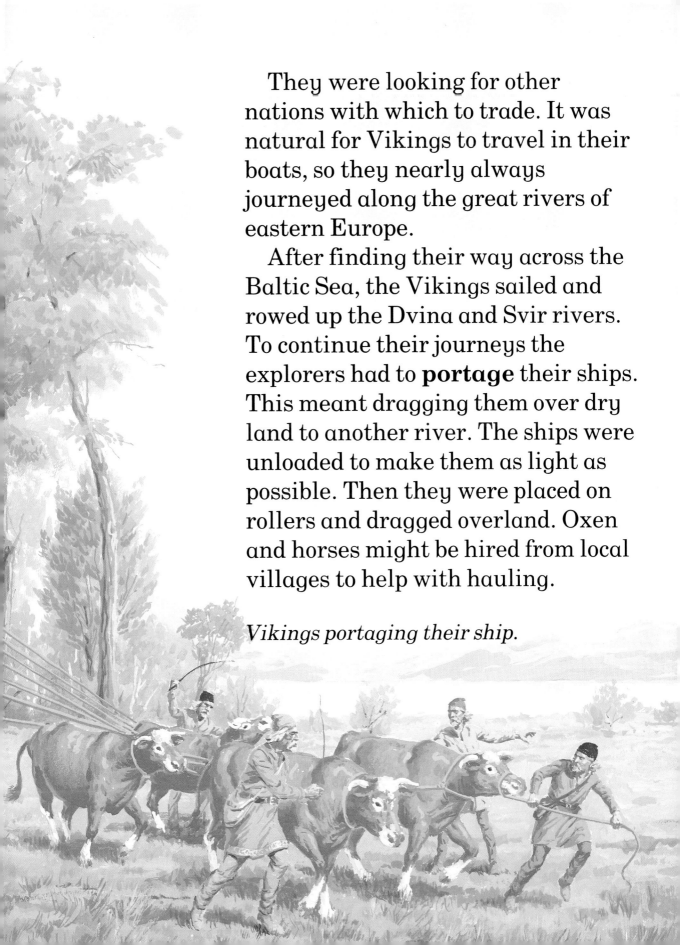

Vikings portaging their ship.

A Viking merchant selling his furs in a town in Asia.

VIKING MERCHANTS

It was at the portages that a Viking merchant would decide where to look for trade. If he travelled down the Dneiper River he would eventually reach the wealthy city of Constantinople. The Volga River would take him to the Caspian Sea and so to Asia.

Whatever route they followed, most Viking merchants carried the same type of goods. The most important of these were furs and **slaves**. Animals with soft fur, such as fox, beaver and squirrel, were caught in Scandinavian forests. Slaves were captured during raids into eastern Europe. The Vikings sold their goods for gold and silver or exchanged them for luxuries such as **silk, spice** and jewellery. Some Viking merchants became very rich through trading.

THE WEALTH OF BIRKA

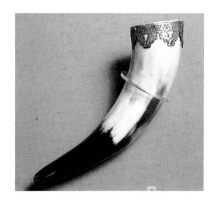

Thousands of Viking explorers, merchants and settlers left Scandinavia. Even when these people did not return, they kept in contact with their homeland. Settlers sent back goods in exchange for tools and weapons, which they could not make for themselves in their new settlements. Merchants constantly travelled from Scandinavia to foreign lands looking for trade.

These merchants made money and gained wealth. The centres for their

Top *A decorated bull's horn, used as a cup.*

Above *A small silver cup.*

Right *Ivory chesspieces, carved from the tusk of a walrus.*

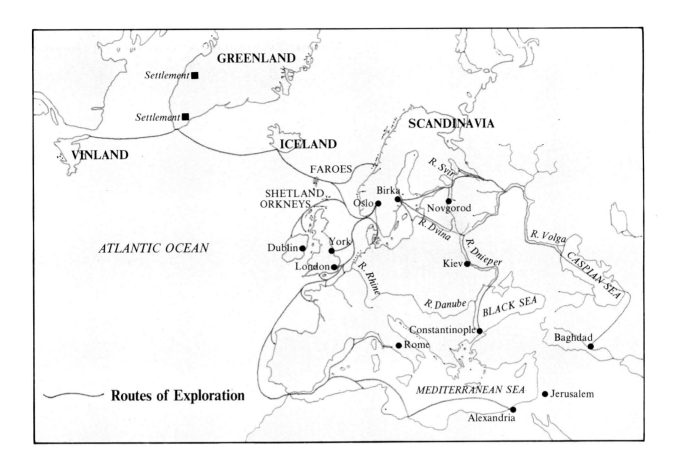

Map labels:

GREENLAND

Settlement ■

Settlement ■

VINLAND

ICELAND

FAROES

SCANDINAVIA

R. Svir

SHETLAND
ORKNEYS

Birka

Oslo

Novgorod

R. Dvina

R. Dnieper

R. Volga

CASPIAN SEA

ATLANTIC OCEAN

Dublin

York

London

R. Rhine

Kiev

R. Danube

BLACK SEA

Constantinople

Rome

Baghdad

— Routes of Exploration

MEDITERRANEAN SEA

Jerusalem

Alexandria

prosperous activities were several towns in Scandinavia. Birka was one of the most important of these towns. Rich merchants lived in or near the town, as did many less wealthy tradesmen. Ships visited Birka from many parts of Europe.

Wherever these courageous explorers settled they introduced skills such as shipbuilding, jewellery, coin and tool making.

A map showing the routes taken by Viking explorers across the sea and along rivers.

21

GLOSSARY

Cargoe Goods carried by ship or other transport

Celtic The people who lived in Wales, Scotland, Ireland and nearby islands.

Feud A quarrel or dispute.

Grazing Grounds Areas of land where there is plenty of grass for animals such as cattle and sheep to eat.

Implements Tools and equipment.

Knarr A cargo ship used by Viking merchants.

Longship A fast ship used by Vikings when they wished to attack other people.

Manoeuvrable Easily managed and able to turn quickly.

Merchant A person who earns a living by buying goods in one place and selling them in another at a profit.

Portage The act of hauling a ship or boat over dry land, or a place where this happens.

Sacred Something that is holy or has religious significance.

Scandinavia The part of northern Europe, in which Norway, Sweden and Denmark are situated.

Silk A very expensive cloth manufactured in China during the Viking Age.

Slave A person who is owned by another and is not free.

Spice A substance such as pepper or cinnamon which has a strong flavour and is used in cooking.

Vinland The Viking name for America. Vines grew wild in the area explored by the Vikings so they called it Vine-land.

BOOKS TO READ

Alfred the Great and the Saxons by Robin May (Wayland, 1985).

Ships of the High Seas by Erik Abranson, (Peter Lowe, 1976).

Viking Raiders by A.Civardi and J. Graham-Campbell (Usborne, 1987).

The Vikings – Great Civilizations by Robin Place (Longman, 1980)

The Vikings by Terence Richard (Wayland, 1986).

A Viking Sailor by Christopher Gibb (Wayland, 1986).

A Viking Settler by Giovanni Caselli (Macdonald, 1986).

Picture acknowledgements

Bruce Colman / Ray Brynant 9 (lower), O. Langrand 10 (lower); Michael Holford 6 (top), 9 (top), 20 (lower left and right); Ronald Sheridan Picture Library 6 (lower), 10 (top), 14 (top and lower), 20 (top). Map on page 21 is by Malcolm Walker.

INDEX